discarded

INSIDE THE WORLD OF SPORTS

TRACK & FIELD

INSIDE THE WORLD OF SPORTS

AUTO RACING

BASEBALL

BASKETBALL

EXTREME SPORTS

FOOTBALL

GOLF

GYMNASTICS

ICE HOCKEY

LACROSSE

SOCCER

TENNIS

TRACK & FIELD

WRESTLING

INSIDE THE WORLD OF SPORTS

TRACK & FIELD

by Andrew Luke

MASON CREST

3

Mason Crest
450 Parkway Drive, Suite D
Broomall, Pennsylvania 19008
(866) MCP-BOOK (toll free)

First printing
9 8 7 6 5 4 3 2 1

ISBN (hardback) 978-1-4222-3467-9
ISBN (series) 978-1-4222-3455-6
ISBN (ebook) 978-1-4222- 8429-2

Cataloging-in-Publication Data on file with the Library of Congress

QR CODES AND LINKS TO THIRD-PARTY CONTENT

You may gain access to certain third-party content ("Third-Party Sites") by scanning and using the QR Codes that appear in this publication (the "QR Codes"). We do not operate or control in any respect any information, products, or services on such Third-Party Sites linked to by us via the QR Codes included in this publication, and we assume no responsibility for any materials you may access using the QR Codes. Your use of the QR Codes may be subject to terms, limitations, or restrictions set forth in the applicable terms of use or otherwise established by the owners of the Third-Party Sites. Our linking to such Third-Party Sites via the QR Codes does not imply an endorsement or sponsorship of such Third-Party Sites, or the information, products, or services offered on or through the Third- Party Sites, nor does it imply an endorsement or sponsorship of this publication by the owners of such Third-Party Sites.

CONTENTS

KEY ICONS TO LOOK FOR:

Words to understand: These words with their easy-to-understand definitions will increase the reader's understanding of the text while building vocabulary skills.

Educational Videos: Readers can view videos by scanning our QR codes, providing them with additional educational content to supplement the text. Examples include news coverage, moments in history, speeches, iconic sports moments and much more!

Text-dependent questions: These questions send the reader back to the text for more careful attention to the evidence presented there.

Research projects: Readers are pointed toward areas of further inquiry connected to each chapter. Suggestions are provided for projects that encourage deeper research and analysis.

Who can run the fastest? Who can jump the highest or throw the farthest? These are the tests of human speed, strength and endurance that comprise the sport of track and field, pushing its athletes to their limits.

CHAPTER 1

TRACK AND FIELD'S GREATEST MOMENTS

In the United States, the sport of track and field barely registers on the public radar, other than every four years when the Summer Olympic Games roll around. It is true that every generation has its recognizable names in the sport: Jesse Owens, Bruce Jenner, Carl Lewis, Florence Griffith, Jackie Joyner, Mary Decker, and Michael Johnson. In the 1980s, Mary Decker was on the cover of the venerable sports publication *Sports Illustrated* three times in a four-year span. An American track and field athlete has not been featured on the cover in this century. Among all track and field athletes, only the world's fastest man, Jamaican Usain Bolt, has managed to make the cover since 2000, and he had to run faster than anyone in history to be noticed.

Justin Gatlin might have the most name recognition in U.S. track and field, but not all of it is positive. He served a four-year drug-related suspension in 2006. The prevalence of illegal drug use has tainted the sport in the eyes of many would-be fans.

Nonetheless, there have been plenty of successes to write about and cover, but most Americans would have no idea who Ashton Eaton, Aries Merritt, Christian Taylor, Sanya Richards, Dawn Harper, or Jenn Suhr are. All won individual Olympic gold medals for the United States this century, and four of the six set world records.

America is still competitive in track and field, but the mainstream public sports interest in the country is dominated by football, baseball, and basketball. In Europe, however, Eaton is a household name, and Taylor and Merritt are stars that fans of athletics (as the sport is called there) pay to watch.

In a newspaper interview in 2012, Jenner said, "You have to admit, we've gone up against the marketing machine of football, basketball, and baseball, multibillion-dollar budgets, and in golf, you had a superstar with Tiger (Woods) that has really brought the sport back. We need to find a couple of those kinds of superstars with great personalities, too."

Whether or not the sport can make a comeback in the future remains to be seen, but the stars will keep on running, jumping, and throwing, creating the greatest moments track and field has ever seen.

Owens Owns Berlin

The Summer Olympic Games of 1936 were held in Berlin, Germany, at a time of great unrest. The Nazi party came to power in 1933, and its leader Adolf Hitler saw the event as a platform to showcase the Nazis and their idea of the racial supremacy of Caucasians. American sprinter Jesse Owens had other ideas.

The 100 meter (109 yard) sprint took place on August 3, 1936. Hitler was in attendance for what is considered to be the signature event of the Summer Games. Not only did Owens and fellow black teammate Ralph Metcalfe finish first and second, but Owens also tied the world-record time of 10.3 seconds. Owens would go on to further prove his supremacy by winning three more gold medals.

A Leap for the Ages

American Bob Beamon only won one gold medal in his career, but it was one of the most spectacular in Olympic history. It came at the 1968 Summer Games in Mexico City. Beamon was favored to win the long jump event, having lost only one meet all year.

Beamon had come close to the world record of 8.35 m (27.40 feet) twice that year, jumping 8.33 m (27.33 feet) and a wind-assisted 8.37 m (27.46 feet). Yet no one could have expected what happened on his very first jump of the Olympic competition. Beamon settled himself at the top of the runway, took 19 strides to hit the board perfectly, and soared into history. He leaped an incredible 8.90 m (29.20 feet), beating the existing world record by an astonishing 0.55 m (1.80 feet). It is one of the most impressive records in Olympic history and one that stood for nearly 23 years.

Human Rights Salute

At those 1968 Mexico City Games, Beamon's teammates Tommie Smith and John Carlos made a historic impression of their own. The two sprinters were competitors in the 200 m (219 yard) event, in which Smith was the current world record holder. In the event final, Smith blazed to a new record 19.83 seconds. Carlos finished third to win the bronze medal behind Peter Norman of Australia.

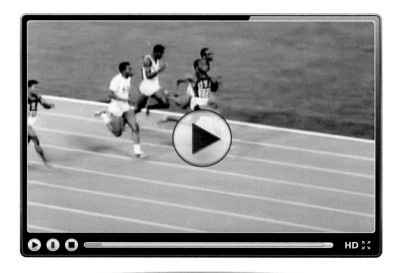

The three medalists then took place in the most eventful medal ceremony in Olympic history. Smith and Carlos, both African American, had been vocal critics of the International Olympic Committee (IOC) and its stance on human rights leading up to the games, especially president Avery Brundage. During the playing of the U.S. national anthem, both men raised black-gloved fists in the air and bowed their heads in a salute intended to draw attention to what they saw as human rights shortfalls in their country and others. All three medalists wore the badge of the Olympic Project for Human Rights.

Decker Versus Budd

Human rights concerns especially centered on the country of South Africa and its policy of apartheid, which discriminated against its black citizens. This continued to be true as the 1984 Olympic Games approached, as South Africa had been expelled from the IOC officially in 1970. Athletes from South Africa had to find other means to compete.

This was the case with Zola Budd, a South African distance runner who qualified to compete for Great Britain. Budd was considered a threat to American Mary Decker in the 3000 m (3,281 yard) event at the 1984 Games in Los Angeles. Decker was the reigning world champion and the heavy favorite, expected to make up for previous Olympic disappointments. She missed the 1976 and 1980 Games due to injury and boycott, respectively. Her greatest disappointment came in the 1984 final, however, as she and Budd collided on the fourth lap, causing Decker to lose her balance and fall. The image of Decker in tears as her medal hopes evaporated is one of the most enduring from those games.

Fighting to Finish

Decker was injured in her fall and did not finish the race. Eight years later at the games in Barcelona, an in-race injury to British runner Derek Redmond also ended his race. The enduring image, however, was a very different one.

Redmond was a medal contender coming into the 400 m (437 yard) semifinal in Barcelona after an injury forced him to withdraw from the Seoul Games in 1988. Redmond was running well down the backstretch when his hamstring popped. He fell to the ground in pain but waved off medical personnel when they ran out to assist him. His father, who was watching from the stands, jumped onto the track and ran out to help his son. Together, the two men walked the final meters, son leaning on father, so Redmond could cross the finish line. The 65,000 spectators gave them a standing ovation.

Double Gold

In Barcelona, American Michael Johnson did not compete in Redmond's event, the 400 m, running only the 200 m and the 4x400 m relay. By the 1996 Olympic Games in Atlanta, however, Johnson was the favorite to win both the 200 m and 400 m events. He came in as the reigning world champion in both events and the world record holder in the 200 m.

The 400 m final came first, which Johnson won in Olympic record time. That set up his attempt to achieve the unprecedented feat of winning double Olympic gold in the 200 and 400 m events. His world-record time coming in was 19.66 seconds. In the Olympic final, the Texan ran a staggering 19.32 seconds, the biggest ever improvement on the 200 m record. Johnson's 200 m record stood for 12 years until it was broken by Jamaica's Usain Bolt in 2008.

Freeman's Glory

At those 1996 Games in Atlanta, Australia's Cathy Freeman won the silver medal in her specialty, the 400 m. Going into the next Olympics on her home soil in Sydney in 2000, Freeman was the favorite in the event as the reigning world champion. She carried the weight of a nation with her. Not only was Freeman the sole medal hope for the home nation in track and field, but she would also be the first Aboriginal person to win a medal as well.

Freeman cruised through qualifying, and in the final of the 400 m she ran a 49.11-second time, the fastest in the world to that date, to win the gold easily. The medal was the 100th gold medal in the history of her country, and more than 100,000 were on hand in Sydney to witness it. She did a victory lap around the track carrying both the Australian and Aboriginal flags.

Watch the video instantly on your mobile device by scanning the QR code next to each video player!

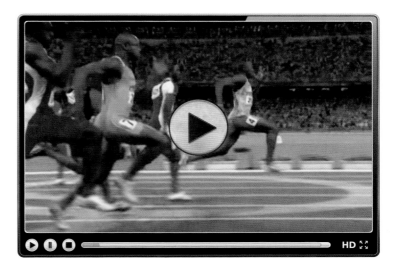

Lightning Bolt

The Jamaican flag has frequently been on display at Olympic track and field venues over the years. The tiny island nation is a sprinting powerhouse and has produced more than 15 gold medals. One of the most memorable came at the 2008 Games in Beijing.

Usain Bolt came into the Beijing Olympics in August 2008 as the world record holder in the 100 m, having broken countryman Asafa Powell's record in May. Bolt's mark of 9.72 seconds was under siege by its owner during the event as Bolt ran 9.85 in the semifinals. In the final he lowered his world record to 9.69 to win the gold in spectacular fashion, finishing a full 0.2 seconds ahead of silver medalist Richard Thompson of Trinidad. Bolt's lead was so great that he began to celebrate 10 m (33 feet) from the finish, which indicated that he could probably go even faster. Jamaica won five of the six sprint gold medals in Beijing.

Running, jumping and throwing are current track and field skills used by the earliest of humans for survival rather than sport.

Words to Understand:

nomadic: anything that involves moving around frequently and over large distances; nomadic hunter-gatherer tribes follow the animals they hunt, carrying tents with them

hieroglyphics: a pictographic script, particularly that of the ancient Egyptians, in which many of the symbols are conventional, recognizable pictures of the things represented

pentathlon: an athletic contest comprising five different track and field events and won by the contestant gaining the highest total score

CHAPTER 2

THE HISTORY OF TRACK AND FIELD

The acts of running, jumping, and throwing are as old as humankind. For primitive humans, however, these acts had much more practical purposes, primarily self-preservation.

SURVIVAL SKILLS

Running away or throwing rocks were the only means of defense when early humans were threatened by attacking animals or by other humans. Rather than survival of the fittest, it was survival of the fastest.

In the Stone and Bronze Ages, people developed slightly more sophisticated weapons, such as slings and spears, which allowed them to move from foraging for berries and plants to hunting.

TO THE HUNTERS GO THE SPOILS

Members of the tribe that proved best at the skills required for hunting were honored with the best lodging and food. Speed in pursuit of prey and throwing spears, rocks, or flat stones to bring down animals are the modern-day equivalents of the sprinting, javelin, shot put, and discus events in track and field.

Even as humans evolved and settled into communities that primarily raised crops, hunting was still necessary to provide protein for the tribe. The hunters also became the defenders of these now stationary communities that were easier to target than in their previous **nomadic** forms.

WARRIOR SKILLS

As hunting skills became warrior skills, tribe members who excelled at them were celebrated among their people. The worship and adoration heaped upon athletes in modern society are very similar to how primitive warriors were treated by their own tribes. Cave drawings and **hieroglyphics** from ancient civilizations depict the stories of these warriors much like books and video tributes do the stories of Jesse Owens or Carl Lewis today.

Barnard College Greek Games statue

BARNARD GREEK GAMES

Which of the tribe's warriors should be most celebrated? This is a question that arose naturally as the human traits of jealousy and competition came into play. Receiving the most glory and the highest honors became prizes to vie for. The competitions of track and field evolved not from children's games, as some had once theorized, but rather from the importance of running and throwing skills to tribal societies. The question of which warrior was the fastest or most talented was settled with a race or a contest of skill.

PLEASING THE GODS

The worship of multiple gods was common among most ancient tribes and civilizations, from primitive to advanced. To honor and gain the favor of these gods, festivals were often held in their names. Contests of speed, strength, and skill were held at these festivals that would attract thousands of spectators.

Games of skill were also contested at the funerals of chiefs or leaders to properly commemorate their departure from the mortal world. Spectators at these events would boo and cheer the efforts of the competitors just as we do at sporting events today.

GREEK GAMES

Of the ancient civilizations, it is the Greeks who are best known for organizing and conducting games of speed and skill. They documented competitions such as distance races, broad jumping, javelin, and discus throwing as well as events like chariot races, wrestling, and archery.

Cities across the Greek empire conducted these games, and athletes would travel from city to city to compete. Gradually, certain festivals or competitions gained higher levels of prestige, and eventually the competition at the city of Olympia emerged as the site of the most prestigious Greek games. They were held every four years as a tribute to Zeus, king of the gods.

OLYMPICS

Games at Olympia, a longtime shrine to Zeus, had taken place for hundreds of years before the first known written records from 776 BC. As these games grew into the spectacle that became the Olympics, winning at Olympia gave an athlete enormous popularity, allowing him to garner invitations from other major events, much like a win at the Olympics today gives athletes exposure and prestige that allows them to command appearance fees and sponsorships.

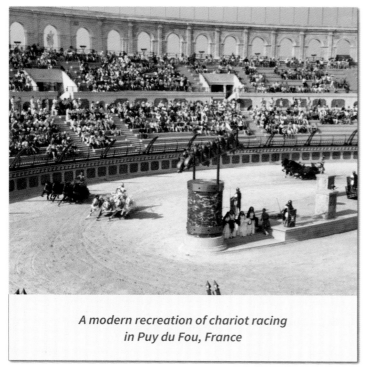

A modern recreation of chariot racing in Puy du Fou, France

The Olympic Games continued for thousands of years, and as they grew, stadiums were built along with housing for the athletes. The Olympics were a must-see event known across the Greek empire. The chariot races probably provided the biggest spectacle, but it was the athletes of the **pentathlon** who captured the highest praise. The test of strength and skill included the discus and javelin throws, a standing broad jump, a 200 m race, and a wrestling match.

NO WOMEN ALLOWED

The Olympic Games, like all things of importance or prestige in ancient Greek society, were exclusively for men. To prevent disguised women from trying to compete, athletes competed naked. There is a story that the mother of an athlete disguised herself as a trainer, so she could watch her son compete, and when she was discovered, trainers also had to attend events wearing nothing.

Though never allowed to compete in the original Olympics, women around the Greek empire did stage their own competitions in other locations, consisting of wrestling, chariot races, and foot races.

THE FALL OF OLYMPIA

After the Romans conquered the Greeks, the games at Olympia lost their influence to competitions in other less remote and more populated locations. The Romans also actively discouraged non-Roman forms of worship, and Zeus-centered Olympia became even further isolated.

In the fifth century, the original Olympic Games ceased to exist, and a series of sixth-century earthquakes are believed to have eventually destroyed the last Olympic buildings.

Ruins of the Philippeion in Ancient Olympia (Greece)

Text-Dependent Questions:

1. In the Stone and Bronze Ages, people developed slings and spears which allowed them to move from foraging for berries and plants to what?

2. Which of the ancient civilizations documented competitions such as distance races, broad jumping, javelin, and discus throwing as well as events like chariot races, wrestling, and archery?

3. To prevent disguised women from trying to compete in the Olympics, how did athletes compete?

Research Project:

As we learned in this chapter, the worship of multiple gods was common among most ancient tribes and civilizations, and to honor and gain the favor of these gods, festivals were often held in their names. Contests of speed, strength, and skill were held at these festivals that would attract thousands of spectators. Through internet searches or books in your library, learn more about these various festivals. Make a collage showing the kinds of skill contests held at the events and the prizes awarded to the winners.

With the 1908 Olympic Games taking place in London, the United Kingdom team, seen here at the opening ceremonies, entered 676 competitors, nearly double the number sent by any other country.

Words to Understand:

superiority: the quality or state of being high or higher in quality

abolitionist: principles or measures to end or stop something, for example, slavery

prevalent: common, accepted, done or happening often or over a large area at particular time

CHAPTER 3

MODERN ATHLETICS

The Olympics may have disappeared, but the element of competition in human nature persisted through the centuries. When not at war with each other, people's personal, regional, and even national pride led to peaceful competitions to determine athletic **superiority** and the accompanying bragging rights.

ATHLETICS IN AMERICA

For some groups of people, athletics was the only means of expressing superiority. From the 17th into the 19th century in what is now America, slavery was the law of the land, and black slaves had no rights or freedoms under that law. They did have athletics. As former slave and **abolitionist** Frederick Douglass wrote, slaves spent their free time "in sports, ball playing, wrestling, boxing, and foot racing." Slave children took pride in besting the children of their masters in running and jumping.

As running and even walking races became popular in the newly founded United States, promoters would be careful to include deliberately a racial mix in the competitors they invited. In the North, this meant the spectacle of races between black, white, and Native American competitors.

ATHLETIC CLUBS

In post-Civil War America, organized racing continued to grow, and the methods of and ideas about training expanded along with it. Social clubs formed to provide top athletes with training facilities, living expenses, and coaching. These clubs were typically for whites only.

The Amateur Athletic Union (AAU) was formed in 1888. This group eventually came to set the standard for track and field competitions in the United States, although clubs continued to hold their own meets.

COLLEGE ATHLETICS

College-level track and field meets began in 1873, mostly consisting of long-distance racing. When the Intercollegiate Athletic Association of the United

Athletics event in Detroit Athletics Club in 1888

States (later the National Collegiate Athletic Association [NCAA]) formed in 1906, it organized regional and national meets.

In the North, black athletes were welcome at integrated schools, and integrated meets have been held since 1895. In the South, however, black colleges staged and competed in their own meets.

THE FATHER OF THE GAMES

Pierre de Coubertin was born in Paris, France, in 1863. The 5'3" (1.6 m) Frenchman was no athlete but, rather, an academic and an educator. During travels to observe schools in England in 1886, he became convinced of the importance of physical education, **prevalent** in British schools but not taught in France. He believed organized sport created social strength and built morals but could never get the idea to take hold in France. He soon turned this failure, however, into an effort to create an international festival of athletics.

Pierre de Coubertin

De Coubertin had visited the archeological digs at Olympia that were uncovering the ancient Olympic buildings earlier that decade, so in 1889, he began his effort to revive the Olympic competition. He believed the games should be for amateurs only and spearheaded the organization of amateur athletic societies into the Union des Sociétés Françaises de Sports Athlétiques (USFSA). The union started with seven societies and 800 members in 1889 but expanded to 62 societies and more than 7,000 members strong by 1892.

THE MODERN OLYMPICS

At the annual USFSA meeting in 1892, de Coubertin first publicly suggested the idea of reviving the ancient Olympic Games, but the notion received little support. Over the next two years, de Coubertin worked tirelessly on his idea while publicly downplaying his enthusiasm for it. A congress on amateur sport was organized at the Sorbonne in Paris in 1894. Of eight articles on the pre-circulated agenda, seven had to do with the idea of amateurism and only one with reviving the Olympics.

When participants arrived, however, they were divided into two commissions, one on amateurism and one on Olympic revival. Out of this congress came the proposals that the games be held every four years and should consist of modern sports (there would be no chariot racing). The first two locations were chosen. Olympia was considered but abandoned for Athens instead as Olympia was too remote and had limited infrastructure. Paris, for the 1900 Games, was the second location. Out of the congress, the International Olympic Committee (IOC) was formed, headed by Demetrius Vikelas of Greece.

Olympic Games, 1896; preparation for the 100-meter race

THE GAMES BEGIN

The United States sent a 10-person delegation to the 1896 Olympic Games in Athens. American James Connolly won the very first gold medal to be awarded with his victory in the triple jump. His teammate Bob Garrett won two gold and two silver medals. In fact, Americans won nine of the 12 track and field events.

The 1900 Olympic Games in Paris were a relative disaster. The French were indifferent to the idea of the games, and in an effort to boost interest, they were scheduled in conjunction with the five-month-long 1900 World's Fair. The IOC allowed an organizing committee associated with the fair to control the planning. Poorly prepared venues and last-minute scheduling changes were the result. American Ray Ewry managed to win three jumping events in the chaos. The 1904 Games were held in St. Louis and also organized around an international exposition. They were not well attended by either athletes or spectators. Americans made up 80 percent of the athletes. The English, who had dominated the non-sprint track events in Paris, did not send a single competitor; nor did the French, to de Coubertin's dismay.

Text-Dependent Questions:

1. What union was formed in 1888 and eventually came to set the standard for track and field competitions in the United States?

2. Who is known as "the Father of the Games"?

3. The 1896 Olympic Games were held in what city?

Research Project:

Take a closer look at the life of Pierre de Coubertin and his role in reviving the Olympics. Compare the first several Olympic Games in terms of athletes attending from various countries and spectator turnout. Share your thoughts on the growing pains endured in the process of bringing back the Olympics to a modern-day success.

The opening ceremony in the Panathinaiko Stadium, 1896 Olympic Games

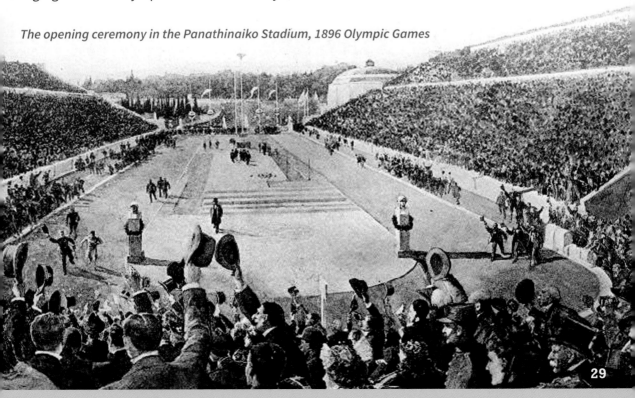

Twenty-five countries sent athletes to compete in events like the 110 m hurdles at the 1912 Olympic Games in Stockholm, Sweden.

Words to Understand:

dramatic: attracting attention, causing people to listen carefully and look

delirious: not able to think or speak clearly, especially because of fever or other illness

Aryan: used in Nazism to designate a supposed master race of non-Jewish Caucasians usually having Nordic features

CHAPTER 4

THE OLYMPICS: TRACK AND FIELD'S LIFEBLOOD

Desperate to revive the games after two debacles, de Coubertin proposed returning to Athens every four years between the official Olympic Games. In 1906, the Second International Olympic Games in Athens (now referred to as the Intercalated Games) were held to tremendous enthusiasm and success. The United States organized its first official, publicly funded team that actually traveled and trained together. For previous events, athletes trained separately at their respective schools. A record number of countries and athletes took part, and Americans won 11 of the 19 track and field events.

POSITIVE MOMENTUM
Due to unrest in Greece, the Athens Games were not held in 1910 and were then dropped altogether. Even though they are not recognized as official Olympic Games, their importance in restoring the Olympic movement cannot be overstated.

With the momentum of the Athens Games to build from, the 1908 Games in London, England, saw 22 countries send teams. This number increased steadily over the decades. Three games were canceled due to war (1916, 1940, and 1944), but by 1936, 49 countries attended, and in 1956 72 nations sent athletes. Mexico City hosted 112 countries in 1968, and 160 attended in Seoul in 1988. In 2012, more than 200 nations sent more than 10,000 athletes to the Summer Olympics in London.

THE MARATHON
The Olympic Games have been very popular with spectators as well. Overall TV viewership for the 2012 London Games broke records all over the world. Fans especially were drawn to the track and field events. For the London Games, the most watched event on television was the men's 100 m final, won by

The runners leave the stadium after the start of the marathon at the 1912 Summer Olympics.

Jamaican Usain Bolt. That highly **dramatic** and easily digestible 10 seconds is one of the most compelling in sports. Other track events are more difficult to sell on television, such as the more than two-hour marathon races.

The marathon, however, is an important part of the history of the modern games. It was not actually included in the ancient version, which is surprising given the ancient origin in the legend of Pheidippides and his run from the Battle of Marathon in 490 BC. In the story, the courier Pheidippides is sent from the battlefield at Marathon to Athens to proclaim the Greek victory over the Persians. He runs the 42 kilometers (26 miles) and dies after delivering his message. The legend inspired de Coubertin to propose a race of the same distance for the 1896 Games, which given its root in Greek lore, organizers embraced.

EARLY STORIES

The Greeks, who finished first, second, and third, led by winner Spirido Loues, swept the first Olympic marathon in history. Following that first race, the event was drama filled over the next several games.

- In 1900, American Arthur Newton took over the lead at the midway point and pulled away as the race wound its way through Paris. Inside the stadium, at the finish line, stood Frenchman Michel Theato, the race winner. Newton protested that no other runners had passed him. As it turns out, four others finished ahead of him, Theato by more than an hour. Newton had likely taken a wrong turn or two on the poorly marked course.

- In 1904, New Yorker Fred Lorz was exhausted just nine miles (14.5 km) into the race. He hitched a ride in his manager's car for 11 miles (17.7 km), got out, and ran the last six to cross the finish line first. He was discovered and disqualified before the medals were awarded.

- In 1908, Italian Dorando Pietri was leading but struggling badly when he entered the stadium in London for the final lap. **Delirious** with exhaustion, he began running the wrong way. After being redirected by officials, he ran toward the finish but collapsed on the track several times. American John Hayes then entered the stadium and headed for the finish line. The British race officials kept helping Pietri up and eventually carried him over the finish line. In the end, Pietri was disqualified, and Hayes declared the winner.

THE WORLD'S FASTEST HUMAN

In the 1920s, Texan Charley Paddock was the fastest man in the world, which at the time meant he had recorded the fastest times in the 100 yard (91 m) dash. His trademark was to jump in the air over the finish line rather than to run through it. This flying finish made him popular with the press, which dubbed him 'The World's Fastest Human.'"

Paddock often feuded with the AAU over his off-track activities and was frequently suspended from amateur meets for activities the AAU felt were not in keeping with an amateur, such as being paid for writing newspaper articles about the sport. He was allowed to run in the Olympics, however, where he won three medals, including the 100 m gold medal in Antwerp in 1920. He won one more medal in Paris in 1924.

Charley Paddock

WOMEN COMPETE

Sixteen-year-old Betty Robinson nearly missed the bus to high school one morning in her hometown of Riverdale, Illinois, in 1928. She had to break into a full-on sprint to catch it, and the high school track coach happened by to watch the whole thing. He asked her to try out for the track team. Three races

Babe Didrickson

Jesse Owens

later, Robinson was headed to the Olympics in Amsterdam for the debut of women's events at the games. The teenager won the gold medal in the 100 m sprint.

At the 1932 Olympic Games in Los Angeles, it was another woman who delivered standout performances in both track and field events. Mildred "Babe" Didrickson won the 80 m (87 yard) hurdles by running a world-record time of 11.7 seconds. She also won the javelin event and added a silver medal in the high jump as well.

JESSE OWENS

The 1936 Summer Olympics in Berlin are best remembered for the performance of Alabama native James "Jesse" Owens. Owens won four gold medals with victories in the 100 m, 200 m, 4x100 m relay, and long jump events. This triumph had political as well as athletic significance.

The host Germans won more medals than any other country, with 89 to America's second-best total of 56. Owen's medals, however, came in the premier events, ones where Hitler had hoped to show **Aryan** dominance. Today, the track and field events at the Olympic Games represent the pinnacle of the sport just as they did in 1936 Berlin. Athletes compete and train year after year in hopes of achieving glory in those fleeting moments that occur once every four years.

Text-Dependent Questions:

1. Overall TV viewership for what Olympic Games broke records all over the world?

2. Name the sixteen-year-old girl who nearly missed the bus to high school one morning in her hometown of Riverdale, Illinois, and due to her full-on sprint to catch it, ended up being recognized for her talent and later took home the gold medal in the 100 m sprint during the Olympic Games.

3. Who won four gold medals with victories in the 100 m, 200 m, 4x100 m relay, and long jump events in the 1936 Summer Olympics?

Research Project:

In the 1920s, Texan Charley Paddock was the fastest man in the world. Who has he passed that torch onto over the years? Create a chart to compare how "the fastest man in the world" has changed over the years as technology and training methods have improved.

Bob Mathias at the Helsinki Olympics 1952

 Words to Understand:

reigning: the period of time during which someone or something is the best or the most important, powerful, etc.

decathlon: a composite contest that consists of the 100-meter, 400-meter, and 1500-meter runs, the 110-meter high hurdles, the javelin and discus throws, shot put, pole vault, high jump, and long jump

increment: a usually small amount or degree by which something is made larger or greater

CHAPTER 5

POST-WAR PIONEERS

World War II forced the cancelation of the 1940 and 1944 Olympic Games. The Olympics returned with the 1948 Games in London, with Germany and Japan banned.

MIGHTY MAMA

Dutch mother of two Fanny Blankers-Koen was the star of the Games in London, winning gold in four events. Dubbed "The Flying Housewife," 30-year old Blankers-Koen won the 100 m and 200 m sprints, the 80 m hurdles, and the 4x100 m relay.

At the time, Blankers-Koen was also the **reigning** world record holder in both the long jump and the high jump. Women, however, were limited to compete in no more than three individual events; otherwise, she may well have won six gold medals.

DOMINANT DECATHLETE

At the other end of the athlete age spectrum in 1948 was California native Bob Mathias. Mathias competed in the **decathlon**, where at just 17 he became the youngest athlete ever to win a track and field medal when he won the event.

By the 1952 Games in Helsinki, Mathias was a strapping 6'3" (1.9 m) and 205 pounds (93 kg), and he easily defended his title, setting a world record of 7,887 points in the process.

SMASHING RECORDS

In 1953, the American Association for Health published an article on the poor state of youth fitness. President Dwight Eisenhower made it a priority to raise awareness about the importance of physical fitness. Among competitive athletes, better nutrition and more effective training methods took hold, and athletes became bigger, stronger, and faster than ever before in America and around the developed world. In track and field, the result was an assault on the sport's record books that has continued over the decades as science and knowledge improve.

In 1954, coming off a fourth-place finish in the 1500 m (1,640 yard) race in Helsinki, Englishman Roger Bannister ran a mile in just 3:59.4, the first person ever to complete the distance in less than four minutes. Before the decade was up, eight other runners would do the same.

In 1956, President Dwight D. Eisenhower established the President's Council on Youth Fitness.

THE VAULTING VICAR

Field records also fell in the 1950s. In 1957, American Bob Gutowski broke the pole vault record when he cleared 4.78 m (15.68 feet), although this was also due to the introduction of flexible fiberglass rather than bamboo or aluminum poles. At the 1956 Melbourne Olympics, Gutowski finished second behind teammate Bob Richards, the gold medalist in the event from Helsinki. Richards, an ordained minister known as the "Vaulting Vicar," is the only man in history to win two gold medals in the Olympic pole vault.

SURPRISING OLYMPIAN

Wilma Rudolph is one of only two American women in history to win the two individual sprint gold medals at an Olympic Games. Born the 20th of 22 children to a family in Bethlehem, Tennessee, Rudolph suffered from polio, which twisted her left leg. She wore a brace on the leg until she was nine and then an orthopedic shoe until she was nearly 12. At the time, no one would have predicted an Olympic sprinting future for Rudolph.

Wilma Rudolph

When she recovered, Rudolph took up sports and was a natural athlete and a very fast one at that. She was a basketball and track star in high school and made the Olympic team in 1956 and 1960. At the 1960 Games in Rome, she won three gold medals, including the 4x100 m relay.

REPEAT CHAMPION

The title of Fastest Woman in the World passed from Rudolph to Georgian Wyomia Tyus at the 1964 Olympic Games in Tokyo. Tyus was a 19-year-old college student when she won the gold medal in the 100 m and added a silver in the relay.

Still only 23, Tyus returned to the Olympics to defend her title in Mexico City in 1968. She had trained hard the last four years and was well prepared—and it showed. She became the first person ever to defend the 100 m title at the Olympics by setting a world record of 11.08 seconds. She then anchored the U.S. women's relay team to another world record in the 4x100 m race.

ANOTHER FLYING FINN

Another repeat champion, Finland's Lasse Virén, is much less heralded than his famous fellow long-distance running countryman, Paavo Nurmi. Nurmi, the original Flying Finn, won nine gold medals in the 1920s, but Virén's feat of back-to-back double wins in the 5000 m (5,468 yard) and 10,000 m (10,936 yard) events is impressive as well.

Virén set world records in both events at the 1972 Munich Games by skillfully employing bend mathematics, the practice of running very tight corners to cut down on actual distance run. The tragic killing of nine Israeli athletes by the Black September terrorist group during the meet overshadowed Virén's efforts and these games in general. In the 1976 Olympics in Montreal, he won both events again. After winning the 5000 m final, he entered and ran the Olympic marathon the next day, finishing fifth.

DALEY DOUBLE

Politics mixed with the Olympics again in 1980, when 65 countries boycotted the games in protest of the Soviet war in Afghanistan. In retaliation, 14 Soviet-bloc countries, joined by Libya and Iran, boycotted the 1984 Games in Los Angeles. At both sets of games, England's Daley Thompson won gold in the decathlon. One of the greatest ever at the event, he set a world record while winning the 1984 gold medal.

LEWIS AND THE LONG JUMP

A one-time world record holder in the 100 m dash, American Carl Lewis's best event may have been the long jump. Lewis won four straight gold medals in the event from 1984 in Los Angeles through 1996 in Atlanta. His greatest performance, however, came at the 1991 World Championships, where he battled countryman Mike Powell.

With his third of six final-round jumps, Lewis soared 8.91 m (29.23 feet), just over Bob Beamon's 1968 world record of 8.90 m set in 1968. The jump was wind-aided, so not eligible for the record, but did count for the competition. Powell responded with

Carl Lewis

his fourth jump, sailing through the air and hitting the pit at 8.95 m (29.36 feet). The wind was minimal, so Powell's jump was a new world record. Lewis saw the best jump of his life lose to the best jump in history. No one but Powell has ever jumped farther than Lewis did that day.

MICHAEL JOHNSON

Lewis won as many Olympic gold medals in 1984 as Dallas native Michael Johnson did in his three Olympic appearances, but at the 1996 Games in Atlanta, Johnson had a meet for the ages. Johnson set the world record at the 1996 U.S. Olympic trials, running 19.66 seconds. In the 200 m Olympic final, sporting custom-made, gold-colored racing shoes, he flew down the track in 19.32 seconds to shatter his own record. No one had ever lowered the record by so large an **increment**. It stood until Usain Bolt of Jamaica broke it at the 2008 Olympics.

Johnson was even better at the 400 m than the 200 m event. At the 1996 Games, he won the gold in Olympic record time, 43.49 seconds. In 1999, at a meet in Seville, Spain, Johnson broke the world record in the event, setting the current mark at 43.18 seconds. The record has only been broken twice since 1968. The next year, Johnson repeated his 400 m win at the 2000 Olympic Games in Sydney.

AFRICAN DISTANCE RUNNERS

African-born runners have dominated world-class distance running since the 1990s. At 5000 m, African-born runners have posted the 25 fastest times in history and won every Olympic gold medal since 1996. The same can be said at 10,000 m, except for the 15th best time, which belongs to American Galen Rupp. The gold medal streak in the 10,000 m goes back to 1988. Theories abound from the advantage of being raised and training at altitude (many champions are from mountainous regions of Kenya and Ethiopia) to the fact that distance runners are idolized in Africa. In 1968, Africans swept the medals in the 10,000 m, and Kenya won its first three gold medals, all in distance running, including the 1500 m win by national hero Kip Keino. One generation later, African runners started to win everything.

Two of Africa's very best competed at the 2004 Olympics in Athens: Morocco's Hicham El Guerrouj, winner of both the 1500 m (where he is the current world record holder) and 5000 m gold medals, and Ethiopia's Kenenisa Bekele, the 10,000 m champion. Bekele was nearly the double gold medalist over El Guerrouj, finishing second in the 5000 m by just 0.2 seconds. Bekele had set the current world record in the event

Hicham El Guerrouj

Lamine Diack

earlier in 2004. The Ethiopian made up for that disappointment by winning both the 5000 m and the 10,000 m at the 2008 Games in Beijing.

SCANDAL

While doping has led to many scandals in the sport, away from the tracks and fields, corruption has become a source of embarrassment for the International Association of Athletics Federations (IAAF). In 2015, French officials arrested former IAAF president Lamine Diack for allegedly accepting bribes to cover up failed drug tests and laundering money.

Diack was president of the IAAF from 1999 to 2015. He is accused of taking more than one million dollars from the Russian track and field federation to cover up several doping cases from that country. The IAAF suspended Russia from international competition in the wake of the scandal.

Despite these issues that have plagued the sport over the years, on the track and on the field, the world's top athletes continue to amaze.

Text-Dependent Questions:

1. Who was dubbed "The Flying Housewife"?

2. In what year did 65 countries boycott the Olympic Games in protest of the Soviet war in Afghanistan?

3. In 2015, French officials arrested which former IAAF president for allegedly accepting bribes to cover up failed drug tests and laundering money?

Research Project:

Research further the 2015 scandal in the IAAF and its effect on both the federation and the Russian athletes who were suspended from international competition.

Aries Merritt

Words to Understand:

steeplechase: a track and field event in which athletes race over obstacles and water

bestowed: to give (something) as a gift or honor

preceded: to happen, go, or come before (something or someone)

CHAPTER

MODERN-DAY STARS

From running fast or running far to jumping high and throwing long, the stars of track and field today compete in a multitude of disciplines that challenge their strength, speed, and endurance. These are the athletes that continue to push the sport to unprecedented levels.

MEN

TRACK

Usain Bolt of Jamaica is the biggest celebrity in the sport and is the fastest human ever to be recorded. Bolt is the world record holder in both the 100 m and 200 m sprint events. In 2008, Bolt broke both the 100 m and 200 m world records and went on to lower both marks again in 2009.

Usain Bolt

Bolt is the only man in history to successfully defend both the 100 m and 200 m Olympic titles, winning both races in 2008 in Beijing and 2012 in London. When he retires in 2017, he will do so as the greatest sprinter in history.

From running fast to running fast while jumping over things, the 100 m hurdles event is the domain of Georgia native Aries Merritt. Merritt came into his own in the event in 2012, winning the Olympic gold medal in London and setting the world record by running 12.80 seconds at a meet in Belgium.

In 2013, Merritt discovered he had a rare kidney disease that would require a transplant. He had the operation three days after winning bronze at the 2015 World Championships on less than 20 percent kidney function.

Stepping up to the middle distances, Kenya's David Rudisha is the man to beat at 800 m (875 yards). He broke his own world record when he ran 1:40:91 to win the gold medal at the Summer Olympics in London in 2012.

The *Wall Street Journal* called Rudisha's Olympic win "the greatest 800 m race ever run." Six other runners also set personal best times in that 2012 final. Rudisha, a two-time world champion, owns six of the eight fastest times ever recorded for the event.

Stretching out even further to the 3000 m steeplechase event, the dominant man is Rudisha's Kenyan teammate Ezekiel Kemboi. Kemboi won an unprecedented four straight World Championship gold medals in the event from 2009 to 2015.

David Rudisha

Kemboi is also a two-time Olympic champion in the steeplechase, winning gold in 2004 at Athens and again in 2012 at London. He is the only man ever to win more than one gold medal in both the Olympics and the World Championships in **steeplechase**.

Extending the distance much further but slowing to a walking pace brings Frenchman Yohann Diniz to the forefront. In race walking, there are two main events, the 20 km (12.4 miles) and the 50 km (31.1 miles). Diniz has set world records in both.

In 2014, at age 36, he broke the world record at 50 km with a time of 3:32:33. In 2015, at 37, he set the world record in the 20 km at 1:17:02, but this record was broken just a week later.

FIELD

America's Ashton Eaton is the world's greatest athlete. That is the unofficial title traditionally **bestowed** upon the reigning Olympic champion in the decathlon, an event that combines 10 different track and field events. Eaton is the world record holder in the event as well.

Ashton Eaton

Eaton followed up his gold medal at the 2012 London Olympics with a gold at the 2013 World Championships. He then defended that title in 2015, breaking his own world record in the process by scoring 9,045 points.

Eaton's strongest event in the decathlon is the long jump, where he has a career-best jump of 8.23 m (27 feet). To put that in perspective, the qualifying distance to compete in the Olympic long jump is 8.20 m (26.90 feet). Long jump specialists like England's Greg Rutherford routinely jump farther than Eaton ever has.

Rutherford's greatest moment came at the 2012 Olympic Games in front of his home country fans in London, where his fourth-round jump of 8.31 m (27.26 feet) held up for the gold medal. After battling a hamstring injury during the 2013 competition, Rutherford also won gold at the 2015 World Championships.

Greg Rutherford

World Championship gold has eluded the world's best pole vaulter, but Frenchman Renaud Lavillenie always makes it exciting. From 2009 to 2015, he has one silver and three bronze medals in World Championship competition. At the Olympics however, Lavillenie was at his best, winning gold in 2012.

Lavillenie's best effort came in 2014, when he became the absolute world record holder, breaking both the indoor and outdoor records of the legendary Sergey Bubka. He cleared 6.16 m (20.21 feet) at a meet in Bubka's hometown, with the Russian legend watching from the stands.

Great Britain's Jonathan Edwards is the world record holder in the triple jump event with a distance of 18.29 m (60.01 feet) set in 1995. Georgia native Christian Taylor has a great chance of beating that in his career. Taylor jumped 18.21 m (59.74 feet) to win the 2015 World Championship, second best all time, and has three of the six best jumps in the event's history.

At just 21, Taylor won the 2011 World Championship. In 2012, he added the gold medal at the Summer Olympics in London.

Joe Kovacs

Allyson Felix

Taylor's teammate at the 2015 World Championships, Bethlehem, Pennsylvania's, Joe Kovacs, also won a gold medal in his event, the shot put. After failing to qualify for the U.S. Olympic team in 2012 or the World Championship team in 2013, Kovacs had a breakthrough season in 2015.

At age 25, Kovacs threw 22.56 m (74.02 feet) at a meet in Monaco in July, the best throw in shot put in 12 years. He capped the season with the World Championship gold.

WOMEN
TRACK

Los Angeles sprinter Allyson Felix has dominated her events at the World Championships since she was a 20-year-old. She won the 200 m in 2005, the youngest ever to win the event, and defended the title in 2007 and 2009.

At the Olympics, however, Jamaica's Veronica Campbell had been her nemesis, edging Felix for the gold in both 2004 and 2008. In 2012 at London, however, Felix finally beat Campbell to win her Olympic gold medal in the 200 m. After an injury during the 200 m at the Worlds in 2013, Felix decided to concentrate on the 400 m in 2015, where she won World Championship gold, becoming the only woman ever to win titles in both the 200 m and 400 m events.

Jamaica's Shelly-Ann Fraser is Felix's biggest competition at 200 m and is the best in the world at 100 m. Fraser won back-to-back 100 m gold medals in the 2008 and 2012 Summer Olympic Games as well as back-to-back 100 m golds at the 2013 and 2015 World Championships. She also won 2009 World Championship gold in the 100 m, the only three-time female winner in history.

Eunice Sum

Zuzana Hejnová

In the 200 m, she won the 2013 World Championship in a race that saw Felix pull up with a hamstring injury.

Moving up to the middle distances, Kenya's Eunice Sum was the top-ranked female in the world at 800 m for 2015, despite missing out on the gold medal at the World championships by just 0.15 seconds. Sum was the 2013 world champion in the 800 m event.

Sum won four of the six Diamond League races in the 2015 season to win her third straight Diamond League title.

From 1500 to 5000 m, there is no woman better than Ethiopia's Genzebe Dibaba. Once known as the sister of three-time Olympic champion Tirunesh Dibaba, Genzebe has shaken off that mantle with her own unprecedented results.

Genzebe is the indoor world record holder in the 1500 m, 3000 m, and 5000 m events, setting all three marks in a 383-day span from February 2014 to February 2015. Genzebe is also the world record holder at 1500 m outdoors. She won World Championship gold at 1500 m in 2015. In February of 2016, Genzebe also smashed the 26-year-old world record for the indoor mile by more than three seconds, running 4:13.31.

Zuzana Hejnová announced herself on the international hurdling stage with a bronze medal effort in the 400 m event at the 2012 Summer Olympic Games in London. Since then the Czech has been the best in the world at that distance.

Hejnová won seven of eight Diamond League events in 2013 to win that title and added the 2013 World Championship gold medal as well. Derailed by injury in 2014, she repeated the trick in 2015 by again winning the Diamond League title and defending her World Championship title.

FIELD

Hejnová's teammate for the Czech Republic, Barbora Špotáková, is a two-time Olympic champion and the world record-holder in the javelin event. Špotáková won gold at both the 2008 Beijing Olympics and the 2012 London Olympics.

Špotáková followed up her gold medal performance in 2008 by throwing a best-ever 72.28 m (237.14 feet) at a meet in Germany later that year. She also has three World Championship medals, including the gold in 2007.

Moving from throwing a spear to throwing a disc, Sandra Perković of Croatia is the woman to watch. She is a three-time European champion in the discus throw. In 2012 at the Summer Olympic Games in London, Perković won the gold medal in the event.

The following season, 2013, Perković added the title of world champion when she threw 67.99 m (223.06 feet), the best distance in the world that season. She set a personal best with a throw of 71.08 m (233.20 feet) at a meet in Switzerland in 2014.

Sticking with throwing, Poland's Anita Wlodarczyk is the best there is at the hammer throw. She is the two-time world champion in the event, winning gold in 2009 and 2015. She also won silver in 2013 behind Tatyana Lysenko of Russia.

Barbora Špotáková

Anita Wlodarczyk

Just weeks prior to her win at the 2015 World Championships, Wlodarczyk set a world record in the event with a throw of 81.08 m (266.01 feet), becoming the first woman ever to throw over 80 m. Wlodarczyk won the silver medal at the 2012 Olympics in London, losing to an Olympic record throw by Lysenko.

There are stars at the non-throwing field events as well. Primary among them is Caterine Ibargüen of Colombia. Ibargüen is a two-time world champion in the triple jump, winning back-to-back titles in 2013 and 2015.

Ibargüen is also her country's record-holder in the high jump and won a 2011 Pan Am Games bronze medal in the long jump. The triple jump is her best event, however, as she **preceded** her double world championships with an Olympic silver medal in 2012 and a World Championship bronze medal in 2011.

Like Ibargüen, Tianna Madison is skilled in several disciplines and not just in summer sports. Madison grew up near Cleveland, competing in track and basketball.

Long jump was her specialty, and in 2005 at age 19 she won the World Championship gold medal in the long jump and added the World Indoor title the following year. In 2012, she made the U.S. Olympic team in the 100 m dash event and won a gold medal as part of the 4x100 m relay team. She was also a member of the 2012 U.S. Bobsled team. Madison returned to the long jump in 2015, once again winning World Championship gold.

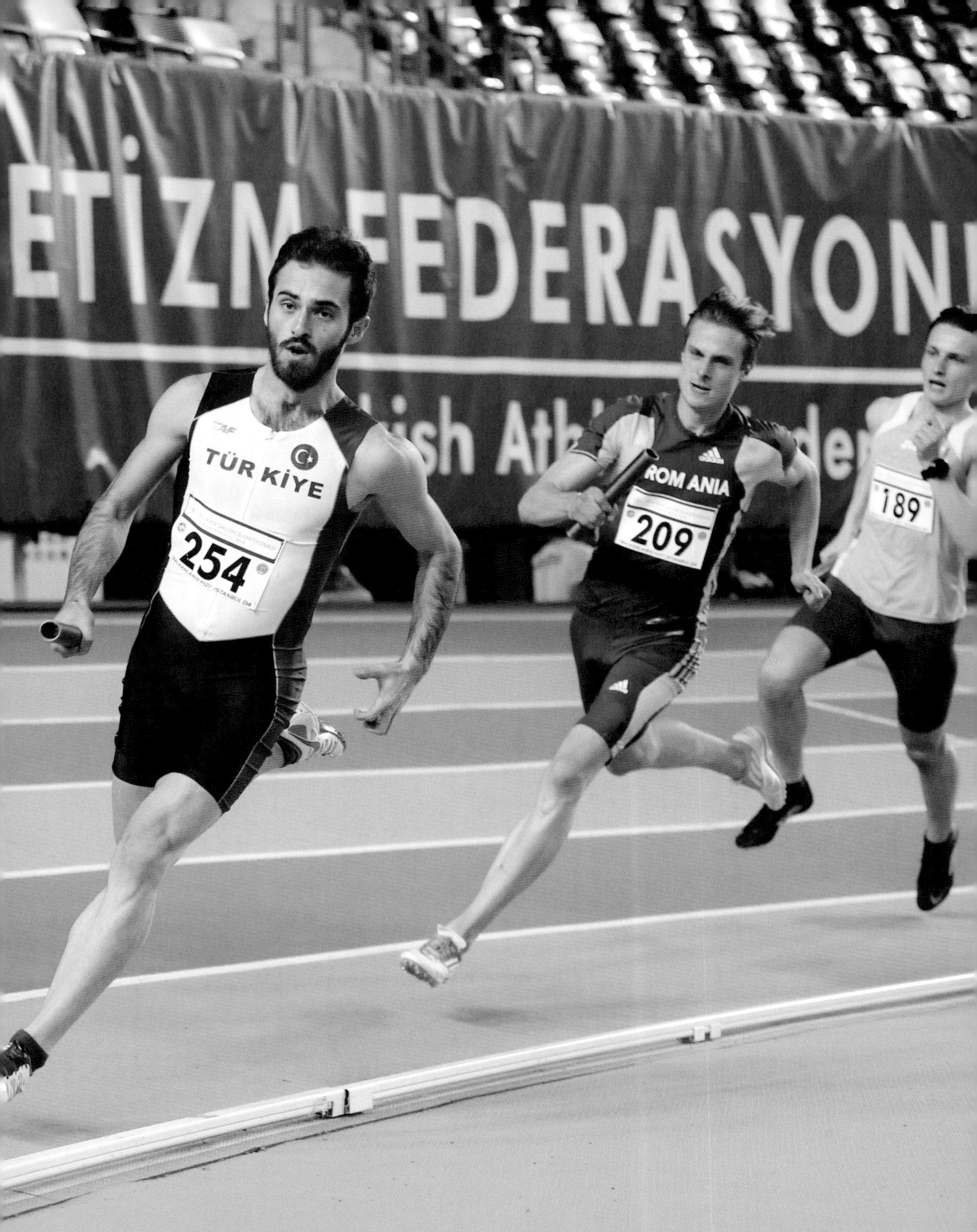

ETİZM FEDERASYON
TÜRKİYE
254
ROMANIA
209
189

Text-Dependent Questions:

1. In 2012 what did The Wall Street Journal call Kenya's David Rudisha's Olympic win?

2. Which Pennsylvania native had a breakthrough season in 2015 and ended up winning a gold medal in his event, the shot put, in the World Championships?

3. Who won back-to-back 100 m gold medals in the 2008 and 2012 Summer Olympic Games as well as back-to-back 100 m golds at the 2013 and 2015 World Championships?

 Research Project:

After reading about both post-war pioneers and modern-day stars, take some time to compare them to each other. In your opinion, what kind of challenges did track & field athletes in the mid-1900s face compared to those of today? How has the rise of the internet, social media and sports news coverage changed the way athletes are shown in the public? Do you think it would have been easier to be a post-war star athlete or a modern-day star?

EMIL ZÁTOPEK

CAROLINA KLÜFT

PAULA RADCLIFFE

WILMA RUDOLPH

FLORENCE GRIFFITH

JACKIE JOYNER   YELENA ISINBAYEVA

KENENISA BEKELE

JESSE OWENS (LEFT)

FANNY BLANKERS-KOEN (RIGHT)

PAAVO NURMI

Scan this QR code to visit the IAAF website to learn more about track and field's greatest athletes

CHAPTER 7

TRACK AND FIELD'S GREATEST ATHLETES

From speed to endurance, from strength to agility, fans of track and field watch to be amazed at what the human body can do. Most of the events in this sport are simple: run fast or long, jump high, or throw far. Unlike hitting a baseball, skating as well as we walk, or catching a football, these are things we can all do innately. We just cannot do it like the best in the world can—and like the best of all time have over the decades.

Part of the fascination also comes from the feeling that what we are watching is what the body can do naturally, guided by proper nutrition, training, and technique. That is why the use of performance-enhancing drugs (PEDs) has so tainted the sport. Athletes who have cheated by trying to enhance chemically what the body can naturally do to gain an unfair advantage over their competitors have given track and field a bad reputation.

With advanced testing, famous cheaters like Canada's Ben Johnson, stripped of the gold medal in the 1988 100 m event, or American Marion Jones, forced to return her five medals from the 2000 Olympics in Sydney, were caught. Instead of being listed among the all-time greats, these athletes are disgraced in history and will not appear in this chapter.

It took a long time for the sport to open its eyes to PED use, however, and many believe the record books are tainted. Women's track and field records from the 1980s are especially suspicious, for example. Random drug testing was not initiated until 1988. Track and field records tend to be incrementally broken every few years, maybe in special cases every 10 or even 20 years, like the men's 400 m record. The women's 800 m record is 33 years old and counting. Only once has anyone come within a second of it. The same can be said of the 400 m record, which is 31 years old.

Jarmila Kratochvílová of Czechoslovakia and Marita Koch of East Germany are the respective record holders, hailing from countries where it is now known PED use was rampant at the time.

The best performers in the history of the sport are not tainted by suspicion, failed drug tests or unlikely performances but, rather, are celebrated due to their consistency and dedication to greatness.

MEN

TRACK

Finland's Paavo Nurmi is the original legend of distance running. "The Flying Finn" set 22 world records in his career in distances ranging from 1500 m to 20 km. At one point in his career, Nurmi was the world record holder in each of the mile, 5000 m, and 10,000 m simultaneously. No other runner has ever done that.

Perhaps the greatest, most staggering accomplishment of Nurmi's storied career came at the 1924 Olympics, where he won five gold medals. The five wins are not what is staggering. The amazing thing is that two of those wins came less than two hours apart. Nurmi ran and won the 1500 m and, less than 120 minutes later, also collected the gold in the 5000 m. No other runner will do that again.

The other legend of distance running is Czech runner Emil Zátopek. Starting in 1947, Zátopek set world records at six distances, from 5000 m to 30,000 m (18.6 miles). He developed his notoriously rigorous training methods in the army. He is famously known to have said, "It is at the borders of pain and suffering that the men are separated from the boys."

The Zátopek legend was cemented at the 1952 Olympics in Helsinki, where Zátopek, who had already won the 5000 m and 10,000 m events, decided to enter the Olympic marathon. He had never before run a marathon but won the event easily in Olympic record time. No other runner has ever won those three events in the same Olympics.

The records of Nurmi and Zátopek have long since fallen by the wayside as training and nutrition have been studied and improved over the years. The modern legend of distance running is Ethiopia's Haile Gebrselassie. Haile competed in distances ranging from the 1500 m to the marathon, but his specialty was the 10,000 m, in which he won four straight World Championships from 1993 to 1999.

Like Nurmi and Zátopek before him, Haile was the world record holder at 10,000 m. His mark

Paavo Nurmi

of 26:22.75 set in 1998 was broken by countryman Kenenisa Bekele in 2005. Haile won four straight Berlin Marathons from 2006 to 2009 and set a marathon world record there in 2008 at age 35.

In American track and field history, the strongest tradition comes from sprinting rather than distance running. The most iconic name in American track and field and one of the most famous in the entire sport is James "Jesse" Owens. Owens was a sprinter and long jumper in the 1930s. Born in Alabama, he grew up mostly in Cleveland and went to college at Ohio State University. At a Big Ten Conference meet in 1935, Owens broke or tied four world records in the span of 45 minutes.

Owens' most famous exploit came at the 1936 Olympics in Berlin, where he defied the notions of racial superiority promoted by Adolf Hitler's new Nazi government by winning four gold medals in front of Hitler himself.

The other paragon of American sprinting is another Alabama native, Birmingham's Carl Lewis. In 1984, Lewis came into the 1984 Summer Olympics in Los Angeles as the world's top-ranked sprinter and long jumper and was widely expected to break world records

Emil Zátopek

Haile Gebrselassie

Carl Lewis

Jesse Owens

in as many as three events. He did not disappoint, matching the feat of Jesse Owens by winning the 100 m, 200 m, 4x100 m relay, and long jump gold medals.

Lewis did not set many individual world records and set just one with his teammates in the relay. In 1991, however, Lewis ran his fastest-ever 100 m at the World Championships to set the world record at 9.86 seconds. Though never a world record holder in the long jump, Lewis is one of the best ever at that event, once winning 65 straight meets.

FIELD

Winning consecutive meets was a strength of discus thrower Al Oerter, Jr., especially when it came to the Olympic Games. Oerter, from Long Island in New York, was a 20-year-old college student at the University of Kansas when he made his first Olympic team in 1956. He threw a personal best 56.64 m (185.83 feet) to win the gold in Melbourne.

In Rome in 1960, Oerter threw an Olympic record 59.18 m (194.16 feet) to win his second straight gold. He again set Olympic records to win the gold in both Tokyo in 1964 and in Mexico City in 1968 at the age of 32. Only Oerter and Lewis have ever won four straight Olympic golds in the same individual track and field event.

Ukrainian Sergey Bubka won six straight World Championships in the pole vault during the 1980s and 1990s. From 1983 to 1997 Bubka was unbeatable at the Worlds, winning the

Sergey Bubka *Jan Železný*

first six pole vaulting championships (the World Championships were contested every four years from 1983 to 1991, switching to every other year beginning in 1993).

Bubka broke the outdoor world record 17 times and the indoor record 18 times. Between August 1984 and 2012, there were only a few scant minutes mid-competition in Rome when Bubka was not the world record holder. Olympic glory was more difficult for Bubka, whose gold medal win at the 1988 Games in Seoul was his only Olympic medal.

Olympic glory came much easier for another world record holder, Czech javelin thrower Jan Železný. Železný won medals in four straight Olympic Games, including three gold medals. He is the world record holder in the javelin with an all-time best throw of 98.48 m (323.10 feet). The top five throws in recorded history all belong to Železný.

Železný also had great success at the World Championships in his career, collecting a total of five medals, including three gold. He also holds the event record for that competition at 92.8 m (304.46 feet). Specifications that reduced the flight ability of javelins were introduced twice in Železný's career, yet he always found a way to throw it farther than everyone else.

Javier Sotomayor always found a way to jump higher than everyone else. The Cuban high jump star cleared a 2.40 m (7.87 feet) bar 40 times in his career. Six others have matched that height a total of seven times. Cuban boycotts of the Olympics in the 1980s prevented Sotomayor from being even more highly decorated than he was. His country sat out the 1988 Seoul Games the year he first set the world record at 2.43 m (7.97 feet).

Sotomayor raised the record to 2.44 m in 1989, which is exactly eight feet on the imperial scale. He also set the world indoor record of 2.43 m in 1989. Cuba finally participated in the 1992 Barcelona Olympics, where Sotomayor won gold. He set the current outdoor world record of 2.45 m (8.04 feet) the following year in Spain.

England's Francis "Daley" Thompson set the world record in the decathlon four times. The London native is widely considered to be the best decathlete in history. He won every competition he entered between 1980 and 1987. He first broke the record in 1980 before winning Olympic gold in Moscow and then raised it twice in 1982.

Thompson went on to defend his Olympic title in Los Angeles in 1984, something only Bob Mathias of the United States has been the only other person to do. He set his fourth world record at those games. Thompson was awarded the order of Commander of the British Empire in 2000.

Javier Sotomayor

Francis "Daley" Thompson

WOMEN

TRACK

Before 1987, Los Angeles native Florence Griffith was a sprinter from UCLA who won a silver medal in the 200 m at the 1984 Olympic Games in her hometown. In 1987, she married Olympic teammate Al Joyner and became known as Flo-Jo (a contraction of Florence Griffith-Joyner). Despite having three World Championship medals to go with her Olympic silver, Flo-Jo did not become a household name until she shattered the world record in the 100 m at the 1988 U.S. Olympic trials.

That world record run of 10.49 seconds is widely believed to have been wind assisted, but that was not the case at the Olympic Games in Seoul, where Flo-Jo won both the 100 m and 200 m sprints, setting the world record in the 200 m at an astonishing 21.56 seconds, a time that has never been approached.

Only one other American woman, Tennessee's Wilma Rudolph, has ever achieved the Olympic double triumph in both sprint events. Rudolph pulled off the feat in her second trip to the Olympic Games in Rome in 1960. She had previously competed in 1956 at Melbourne but only ran the 4x100 m relay, winning a bronze medal. That she competed at all is remarkable, given that childhood polio had prevented her from running until age 11.

Florence Griffith

Wilma Rudolph

Fanny Blankers-Koen

Paula Radcliffe

Rudolph went into the Rome Games as a 20-year-old with the experience not to be intimidated by the Olympic stage. She not only won the double but set an Olympic record in the 200 m and won gold in the 4x100 m relay as well.

The first woman to win the Olympic sprint double was Dutch runner Fanny Blankers-Koen. The setting was the 1948 Olympics in London. Blankers-Koen was already 30 years old and a mother of two. She had competed in the previous Olympics in Berlin in 1936, but World War II and motherhood had delayed her athletic endeavors in the interim.

Blankers-Koen went back to training in 1941 after the birth of her son and came into the London Games as a star athlete, having set six world records in various events. She won four gold medals, the first woman ever to do so, winning the 80 m hurdles and 4x100 m relay medals along with the sprints.

At the middle distances, Southern California-raised Mary Decker was the world's best in the 1980s—and one of the best ever. In 1982, she officially became the first woman ever to run the mile in less than 4:20, one of six world records Decker set that year. In 1983, at the first-ever World Championships, she pulled off the "Decker Double" by winning gold in both the 1500 m and 3000 m events. She never won an Olympic medal.

Decker set dozens of U.S. and world records in her career and is still the U.S. record holder in the mile and 3000 m. She is the only person ever to hold every American record from 800 m to 10,000 m. Her 1983 1500 m U.S. record was finally broken in 2015.

In the distance events, England's Paula Radcliffe was a standout in her career. A runner since the age of seven, Radcliffe came to world prominence in the early 1990s and in 1998 and 1999 won back-to-back European Cup 5000 m titles. In 2001 and 2002, she won back-to-back World Cross Country Championships. In 2002, Radcliffe also turned to marathon running and broke the women's marathon world record while winning the Chicago marathon.

Road racing was Radcliffe's strength, and she won a dozen half or full marathons in her career. The pinnacle was the 2003 London Marathon, where she set the current world record on home soil. She also set the current world record at 10 km that year.

FIELD

Like her sister-in-law Florence Griffith-Joyner, Jackie Joyner also set a world record in 1988 that has never been broken. Joyner was a heptathlete and long jump specialist who grew up near St. Louis. In 1984, she competed at the Los Angeles Olympics in the heptathlon, where she won the silver medal. By the 1988 Olympics in Seoul, Joyner was the dominant female athlete in the world and set a world record of 7,291 points to win the gold. She also won gold with an Olympic record in the long jump.

Joyner defended her heptathlon title in 1992 in Barcelona and was also a two-time world champion in that event as well as the long jump.

Jackie Joyner

Joyner's inspiration growing up was Mildred "Babe" Didrickson, the multisport athlete who was the subject of a movie Joyner saw in 1975. Didrickson, a Texan, represented the United States at the 1932 Olympic Games in Los Angeles. She set a world record winning the 80 m hurdles gold medal on the track but excelled at field events as well.

A natural athlete, Didrickson also qualified for the high jump and javelin events. After settling for a silver medal in the high jump, Didrickson made up for it in the javelin throw, where she threw an Olympic record 43.69 m (143.34 feet) to win gold over two German competitors. After the Olympics, Didrikson went on to become one of history's greatest professional golfers.

Stefka Kostadinova   Carolina Klüft

The women's high jump world record when Didrickson competed in 1932 was 1.657 m (5.435 feet). When Bulgaria's Stefka Kostadinova set the high jump record in 1987, she jumped 2.09 m (6.86 feet), a 25 percent improvement. That mark has remained unbeaten since. Kostadinova set the mark at the 1987 World Championships in Rome. She won five indoor and two outdoor World Championships and broke the world record seven times.

Her world record triumph in 1987 came the year before perhaps her biggest disappointment, a silver medal at the 1988 Seoul Olympics. Kostadinova had four attempts to clear 2.03 m (6.66 feet) for the gold, a height she had jumped many times, but failed on all four. After struggling with injuries in 1992, Kostadinova finally claimed Olympic gold in Atlanta in 1996 at age 31.

Sweden's Carolina Klüft was a high jumper as well but only as part of her true specialty, the heptathlon. Klüft was just 20 years old when she won the first of three consecutive World Championships in the event in 2003. Her career-best high jump was a very good 1.95 m (6.40 feet), but long jump was her strong suit (6.97m [22.87 feet]).

After posting her best-ever score to win her third World Championship in 2007, she retired from the heptathlon to concentrate on the long and triple jumps, meaning she did not defend

Yelena Isinbayeva

her 2004 heptathlon Olympic gold medal at the 2008 Games in Beijing. Had she continued in the heptathlon, she very well may have challenged Joyner's world record in the event. Klüft has the second-best score in history, with 7,032 points.

Klüft was arguably one of the greatest overall athletes ever, but Russia's Yelena Isinbayeva is quite simply the greatest female pole vaulter of all time. She is the current world record holder both indoors and outdoors in the event. Isinbayeva first broke the world record as a 21-year-old at an outdoor meet in England in 2003. In 2004, she won the first of her back-to-back Olympic gold medals in Athens with another world-record vault.

Isinbayeva also won three outdoor and four indoor World Championship titles from 2004 to 2013. In 2005 she became the first woman to clear 5 m (16.4 feet) outdoors, and did the same indoors in 2009, the same year she set the current outdoor and absolute world record of 5.06 m (16.60 feet). She retired in 2013 after winning her third outdoor World Championship.

Career Snapshots

Men

PAAVO NURMI 1920–34*

9-time Olympic gold medalist
3-time Olympic silver medalist
22 world records

JESSE OWENS 1935–36*

4-time Olympic gold medalist
8 NCAA championships
5 world records

EMIL ZÁTOPEK 1944–57*

4-time Olympic gold medalist
Olympic silver medalist
18 world records

AL OERTER JR. 1954–80*

4-time Olympic gold medalist
Pan Am Games gold medalist
4 world records

DALEY THOMPSON 1976–92*

2-time Olympic gold medalist
World Championship gold medalist
20 world records

*Denotes this athlete is in the Hall of Fame

CARL LEWIS 1980–97*

9-time Olympic gold medalist
8-time World Championship gold
  medalist
1 world record

SERGEY BUBKA 1981–2001*

Olympic gold medalist
3-time World Championship gold
  medalist
35 world records

JAVIER SOTOMAYOR 1983–2001

Olympic gold medalist
2-time World Championship gold
  medalist
3 world records

JAN ŽELEZNÝ 1983–2006

3-time Olympic gold medalist
3-time World Championship gold
  medalist
3 world records

HAILE GEBRSELASSIE 1990–2015

2-time Olympic gold medalist
4-time World Championship gold
  medalist
20 world records

Women

BABE DIDRICKSON 1932*

2-time Olympic gold medalist
Olympic silver medalist
3 world records

FANNY BLANKERS-KOEN 1935–55

4-time Olympic gold medalist
5-time European Championship gold
  medalist
6 world records

WILMA RUDOLPH 1956–62*

3-time Olympic gold medalist
Olympic bronze medalist
3 world records

FLORENCE GRIFFITH-JOYNER 1980–88

3-time Olympic gold medalist
World Championship gold medalist
2 world records

MARY DECKER 1972-97*

2-time World Championship gold
  medalist
Pan Am Games gold medalist
8 world records

STEFKA KOSTADINOVA 1985–97*

Olympic gold medalist
7-time World Championship gold
  medalist
3 world records

JACKIE JOYNER-KERSEE 1980–2000*

3-time Olympic gold medalist
4-time World Championship gold
  medalist
5 world records

CAROLINA KLÜFT 2002–10

Olympic gold medalist
3-time World Championship gold
  medalist
World Indoor Championship gold
  medalist

YELENA ISINBAYEVA 2002–13

2-time Olympic gold medalist
7-time World Championship gold
  medalist
17 world records

PAULA RADCLIFFE 1986–2015

World Championship gold medalist
3-time World Cross Country
  Championships gold medalist
3 world records

Too many meets outside of the Olympics and World Championships take place in front of sparse crowds. The IAAF is taking steps to improve the way track and field is marketed in the future.

Words to Understand:

specter: something that haunts or perturbs the mind

engagement: greatly interested; involved in activity

CHAPTER 8

THE FUTURE OF TRACK AND FIELD

In 2015, two-time Olympic champion Sebastian Coe of England was elected president of the IAAF, the governing body of track and field (also known as athletics). Coe was one of the best middle distance runners ever, setting more than 10 world records. Coe took over at an exciting, yet challenging, time for the sport.

DOPING

The **specter** of PED use in track and field continues to cast a shadow on the sport. At the 2015 World Championships in Beijing, the men's 100 m final featured four medal hopefuls, three of whom had previously served a PED-related suspension. Only eventual winner Usain Bolt had no drug history. This came in the wake of accusations that the IAAF had covered up suspicious drug tests dating back to the mid-2000s.

One of the biggest issues is not that dopers are not getting caught at major meets but rather that they are getting through to these meets in the first place. Countries like Jamaica, Russia, and Kenya have all demonstrated a decided lack of adequate drug testing at the national level. Coe has vowed to establish an independent anti-doping agency and an IAAF ethics department as he faces the challenge of eliminating not just cheating but also the suspicion of it from the sport.

GROWTH

Another of the issues facing track and field is that it is only thriving in countries that already dominate the sport. The IAAF, however, has 214 members. Only 87 countries have ever won a single track and field medal. With 60 percent of the membership never having been competitive in the sport, there is certainly room for improvement. Coe has promised to grant each member country a minimum of $100,000 over a four-year span as an "Olympic Athletics Dividend" to be used for training, equipment, facilities, and coaching. The primary goal is to encourage future track and field participations in smaller nations.

POPULARITY

With lagging attendance numbers outside of the major international events (World Championships and Olympics), the sport's leaders know more needs to be done to make track and field more marketable to the masses. This is especially true of the younger generation as the average age of track and field fans tends to skew older.

Coe has promised to create a brand-new division within the IAAF tasked solely with increasing **engagement** with young people with the goal of turning them into fans.

2015 IAAF World Championships in Athletics in Beijing

BUFF THE DIAMOND

The IAAF Diamond League was established in 2010 with the goal of raising the global profile of track and field. A series of meets from May to September would expand the sport outside Europe, with incentives increased to ensure the appearance of top stars, who tend to avoid each other outside of major international events. Officials also hoped to focus the program of events to give fans a clear calendar to follow. Athletes also get points based on where they place in each meet, with the leading point earner named the Diamond League Champion at season's end.

Results for the first five years of the Diamond League were mixed. Not all events offer the same prize money, so some draw a better quality of competition than others. Attendance at the various sites also varies wildly. In London and Paris, the meets draw from 50,000 to 80,000 fans. In New York, that number has been less than 3,000. Coe wants to work toward a more uniform structure, getting a major sponsor for the Diamond League, and improving the marketing of the events, especially at the sites that struggle to fill the seats.

STREET ATHLETICS

Innovative marketing ideas for the IAAF could include implementing a series of street athletics, which take athletes out of stadiums and literally have them compete on the streets in city centers. Coe has proposed doing this in major European cities throughout the track and field calendar.

FUTURE STARS

Sharika Nelvis is a Memphis native who specializes in hurdles. She was the 2014 NCAA champion in the 60 m (66 yard) hurdles indoors and the 100 m hurdles outdoors. In 2015

Nelvis ran the fastest time in the world in the 100 m hurdles, posting a 12.34 second mark.

Nelvis completed her first Diamond League season in 2015, winning meets in Rome and Monaco. She was a favorite to medal at the 2015 World Championships after running the second-fastest time in the semifinals but pulled up with an injury mid-race in the final.

Jaheel Hyde is also a hurdles specialist but is from sprinting powerhouse Jamaica. At age 17, he won the World Junior Championship in the 400 m hurdles in 2014 and is the world youth record holder at the 110 m (120 yard) distance in the hurdles as well. He ran 12.96 seconds at the Nanjing Youth Olympic Games in 2014.

In March of 2015, he set a Jamaican junior record for the 400 m with a 49.01 second time. Hyde turned pro in August of that year.

Sharika Nelvis

Jaheel Hyde

Text-Dependent Questions:

1. Out of the 214 members in the IAAF, how many countries have ever won a single track and field medal?

2. Name one innovative marketing idea that the IAAF could include in future track and field athletics.

3. Who is the up and coming hurdles specialist from Jamaica?

Research Project:

Take to the internet and watch videos of the two future stars mentioned in this chapter. One is American, one is Jamaican, and both are hurdlers. Who do you think is the best? Based on their times and competition in their respective events, which future star do you predict will have the most successful career, and why?

GLOSSARY OF TRACK AND FIELD TERMS

Aboriginal: the native people of Australia, parallel to Native Americans in the United States.

agility: the ability to move quickly and easily.

amateurism: doing something as a pastime rather than as a profession.

boycotted: refused to participate in an event in protest of something.

bragging rights: the ability to say good things about yourself for something you have done.

broad jump: another name for long jump, a track and field event in which athletes run to a spot and then leap as far forward as they can.

comeback: a new effort to succeed after suffering a setback, for example, an athlete competing at a high level after an injury.

discriminated: treated unfairly for belonging to a particular group; discrimination often takes place because of race or gender.

discus: a track and field event in which athletes throw a heavy, flat, round object as far as they can.

endurance: the ability to keep doing something for a long time, even if it requires great strength and concentration.

exposition: a public show, in sports more of a friendly competition.

fitness: a healthy state; in sports, when an athlete's body is in good shape to compete at a high level.

heralded: having stories or news told about someone or something, most often positive.

hurdles: a race in track and field in which runners jump over barriers (hurdles) in their path.

idolized: having admired someone to a great degree or viewed someone as a hero.

javelin: a long spear thrown during a track and field event of the same name.

mainstream: what is popular or widespread at the time; for example, baseball is more mainstream than track and field in the United States.

nemesis: an opponent who is very difficult to beat.

pole vault: a track and field event in which athletes run, jump and use a pole to lift themselves over a crossbar.

prestige: respect and admiration for someone or something for being highly successful.

scandal: something that causes shock because what was done was wrong.

signature event: something unique that helps to define an event or that is promoted as a major part of an event.

shot put: an event in track and field in which athletes throw a heavy ball (about 7 kg [16 lbs.] for men, 4 kg [9 lbs.] for women) as far as they can.

spectators: people who watch an event or competition, the audience.

specialist: a person who has special skill or knowledge in a particular area; in sports, an athlete who focuses on one sport or event.

sponsorship: financial support for a person or organization, usually in return or advertising rights.

steeplechase: a track and field event in which athletes race over obstacles and water.

suspended: kept from participating as a form of punishment; for example, an athlete can be suspended from a sport for using drugs.

unprecedented: not ever having been done before.

CHRONOLOGY

776 BC First written record of an Olympic race is created.

1849 The Royal Military Academy holds the first modern organized track and field meet.

1873 College track competition begins in the United States.

1888 The Amateur Athletic Union is formed.

1896 First modern Olympics takes place in Athens.

1912 Track and field's first international governing body, the IAAF, is formed.

1912 American Jim Thorpe becomes the only man to win both the decathlon and pentathlon in one year.

1932 American Babe Didrikson wins the AAU national team championship as a one-person team.

1936 American Jesse Owens wins four gold medals at the Olympics in Berlin.

1940 American Cornelius Warmerdam is the first to clear 15 feet (4.6 m) in the pole vault.

1954 Englishman Roger Bannister runs first mile in under four minutes.

1968 American Bob Beamon is the first to clear 29 feet (8.8 m) in the long jump.

1976 The Soviet Union's Tatyana Kanzankina becomes the first woman to run the 1500 m event in under four minutes.

1984 American Carl Lewis wins four gold medals at the Olympic Games in Los Angeles.

1985 Ukrainian Sergey Bubka becomes the first man to clear 6 m (19.7 feet) in the pole vault

1988 American Jackie Joyner-Kersee sets the world record in the heptathlon at the Seoul Olympics.

1999 American Michael Johnson sets the world record in the 400 m event at the World Championships in Seville, Spain.

2009 Jamaican Usain Bolt becomes the fastest man in history when he runs 100 m in 9.58 seconds to set a new world record.

2009 Russia's Yelena Isinbayeva sets the world record in the women's pole vault at a meet in Zurich.

2012 Usain Bolt becomes the first man ever to defend both Olympic sprint titles by winning the 100 m and 200 m events at the London Olympics.

Track & Field Today: For the 2016 IAAF World Indoor Championships, the IAAF initiated changes to improve the live spectator experience. In the long jump, triple jump and shot put, the top eight athletes in the 12 athlete final round were traditionally given six attempts. With this meet, the top eight got just five attempts, with only the top four receiving a sixth. All other meet activities stopped while these final four attempts were made, making them the sole focus for the crowd in the arena.

FURTHER READING:

Stanbrough, Marck. *Motivational Moments in 2012 Olympic Track and Field (Motivational Moments in Track and Field)*. Emporia, KS: Roho Publishing, 2013

Hollobaugh, J. *The 100 Greatest Track & Field Battles of the 20th Century.* CreateSpace Independent Publishing Platform, 2012

Schaap, Jeremy. *Triumph: The Untold Story of Jesse Owens and Hitler's Olympics.* New York, NY: Mariner Books, 2008

INTERNET RESOURCES:

International Association of Athletics Federation: http://www.iaaf.org/home

USA Track & Field: http://www.usatf.org/Home.aspx

Olympic Athletics: http://www.olympic.org/athletics

Sports Reference: http://www.sports-reference.com/olympics/sports/ATH/

VIDEO CREDITS:

Owens Owns Berlin (pg 8): https://www.youtube.com/watch?v=QXE6wtvT4sY

A Leap for the Ages (pg 9): https://www.youtube.com/watch?v=ltXXtodzcPY

Human Rights Salute (pg 10): https://www.youtube.com/watch?v=DYeX1bNROJM

Decker Versus Budd (pg 11): https://www.youtube.com/watch?v=5vocnnsNKgU

Fighting to Finish (pg 12): https://www.youtube.com/watch?v=t2G8KVzTwfw

Double Gold (pg 13): https://www.youtube.com/watch?v=JQ9cBQANjiw

Freeman's Glory (pg 14): https://www.youtube.com/watch?v=KOVhDUkmIvk

Lightning Bolt (pg 15): https://www.youtube.com/watch?v=F14EaVEDyUs

International Association of Athletics Federations (pg 54): http://www.iaaf.org/home

QR CODES AND LINKS TO THIRD-PARTY CONTENT

You may gain access to certain third-party content ("Third-Party Sites") by scanning and using the QR Codes that appear in this publication (the "QR Codes"). We do not operate or control in any respect any information, products, or services on such Third-Party Sites linked to by us via the QR Codes included in this publication, and we assume no responsibility for any materials you may access using the QR Codes. Your use of the QR Codes may be subject to terms, limitations, or restrictions set forth in the applicable terms of use or otherwise established by the owners of the Third-Party Sites. Our linking to such Third-Party Sites via the QR Codes does not imply an endorsement or sponsorship of such Third-Party Sites, or the information, products, or services offered on or through the Third- Party Sites, nor does it imply an endorsement or sponsorship of this publication by the owners of such Third-Party Sites.

PICTURE CREDITS

INDEX

In this index, page numbers in ***bold italics*** font indicate photos or videos.